Suddenly
SENIOR

THE FUNNY THING ABOUT
GETTING OLDER

TOM HAY

summersdale

SUDDENLY SENIOR

This edition copyright © Summersdale Publishers Ltd, 2016
First published in 2010
Reprinted 2011 and 2013

Illustrations by Ian Baker

An Hachette UK Company
www.hachette.co.uk

Summersdale Publishers Ltd
Part of Octopus Publishing Group Limited
Carmelite House
50 Victoria Embankment
LONDON
EC4Y 0DZ
UK

www.summersdale.com

Printed and bound in the Czech Republic

ISBN: 978-1-84953-920-3

CONTENTS

EDITOR'S NOTE

You're old enough to have seen life begin at forty, you've faced the big five-O with a frolic and seen in your sixtieth with a smile.

Officially attaining senior citizen status and being awarded a free bus pass might seem to some the last landmark celebration to be enjoyed in later life. But, having wrestled with middle age, we must remember that from here on in it's all downhill in the nicest possible way; a time to kick back, relax and, in the words of William Shakespeare, 'With mirth and laughter let old wrinkles come.' This book, a hearty tonic of wit, wisdom and wisecracks, will help you keep a spring in your step and a song in your heart (albeit a golden oldie), giving you a (somewhat creaky) leg-up to enjoying the brighter side of feeling suddenly senior. So read on and, as you do, don't be too alarmed when you start to feel a twinkle in your wrinkle!

ACHY BREAKY PARTS

I'm at an age where my back goes out more than I do.

Phyllis Diller

I don't need you to remind me of my age. I have a bladder to do that for me.

Stephen Fry

....

One morning, while lying in bed, an elderly man leans over to kiss his wife when all of a sudden she shouts, 'Don't touch me – I'm dead!'

'What are you talking about?' says the husband.

'I'm definitely dead,' replies the wife.

'What in the world makes you think you're dead?'

'I woke up this morning and nothing hurts!'

....

As for me, except for an occasional heart attack, I feel as young as I ever did.

Robert Benchley

Like a lot of fellows around here, I have a furniture problem. My chest has fallen into my drawers.

Billy Casper

....

An old fellow meets the woman of his dreams. When he plucks up the courage to propose, he gets down on one knee and tells her there are two things he would like to ask. 'First,' he says, 'will you marry me?' The woman replies, 'Yes! Yes, I will!' and awaits his second question eagerly. 'That's wonderful!' he cries. 'Now for my second question: will you help me up?'

An ageing gent visits his doctor for a check up. A few days later the doctor sees him walking along the street with a stunning young lady on his arm. A week passes and, on his follow-up visit, the doctor says to the man, 'You're doing well, aren't you?'

'Just doing what you told me to, doc,' the patient replies. 'Get a hot mama and be cheerful.'

'Actually, I said, "You've got a heart murmur, be careful".'

A recently retired gentleman applies for his state pension. After waiting in line for quite a long time, he arrives at the counter. The clerk asks him for his identification to verify his age. The man looks in his pockets and realises he has left his wallet at home. 'Will I have to go home and come back?' he asks. The woman pauses and then says, 'Unbutton your shirt please, sir.' The man opens his shirt, revealing lots of curly silver hair. The woman says, 'That silver hair on your chest is proof enough for me,' and processes his application. When he gets home, the man excitedly tells his wife about his experience, to which she replies, 'It's a good job you didn't take one of your blue pills before you went – if she'd asked to see any more of you she'd never have believed you're sixty-five!'

....

They say that age is all in your mind. The trick is keeping it from creeping down into your body.

Anonymous

I don't deserve this award, but I have arthritis and I don't deserve that either.

Jack Benny

....

An irate customer calls up her local newsagent and demands to know why her Sunday paper hasn't arrived. 'I'm sorry, madam,' the newsagent calmly informs her, 'but I'm afraid today is Saturday. The Sunday paper is not delivered until Sunday.' There is a long pause on the other end of the phone, before the lady replies, 'And I'll bet that's why no one was in church today.'

....

I complain that the years fly past, but then I look in a mirror and see that very few of them actually got past.

Robert Brault

The problem with beauty is that it's like being born rich and getting poorer.

Joan Collins

....

A senior lady goes to the doctor complaining of a range of aches and pains. After examining her, the doctor feels he should be frank: 'Well, Mrs Smith, I'm sorry to say that the aches and pains you're getting are all part of the natural ageing process. I'm afraid I can't prescribe anything to make you younger.' To which she replies, 'I'm not so worried about getting younger, I'd just like you to help make sure I get a little bit older!'

....

You know you're getting old when you can pinch an inch on your forehead.

John Mendoza

An ageing playboy visits his doctor after a lifetime of wine, women and song. 'Well,' says the doctor, 'the good news is you don't have to give up singing.'

I was getting dressed and a peeping tom looked in the window, took a look and pulled down the shade.

Joan Rivers on getting old

....

A retired woman is complaining to her friend about the amount of housework she has to do: 'I spend all day washing, ironing, cleaning, doing the dishes...' she says. 'But what about your husband?' asks her friend. 'My husband? No – I make him wash himself.'

....

I don't feel old. I don't feel anything until noon. Then it's time for my nap.

Bob Hope

Alf and Vera, a couple in their sixties, are holidaying in America. Alf has always wanted some authentic American cowboy boots, so he treats himself to a pair. Back at the hotel, he puts them on and walks into the bedroom and says to his wife, 'Notice anything different about me?' After looking him up and down she shakes her head. Frustrated, Alf storms off into the bathroom, undresses and walks back into the room completely naked except for his beloved boots. Again he asks, a little louder this time, 'Notice anything different about me *now*?' Vera looks him up and down and says, 'Alf, what's different? It's hanging down today, it was hanging down yesterday, it'll be hanging down again tomorrow!'

. . . .

As you get older, the pickings get slimmer, but the people don't.

Carrie Fisher

I refuse to think of them as chin hairs. I think of them as stray eyebrows.

Janette Barber

I guess I don't mind so much being old, as I mind being fat and old.

Peter Gabriel

....

Early one evening, a police car pulls up in front of Grandma Rose's house. She looks out of her window and is shocked to see her husband being escorted out of the car by a police officer. She meets them at the door and is soon relieved to hear that her husband hasn't been up to mischief, but had become lost while trying to find his way home from the pub. 'Oh, Stanley,' says Rose. 'You've been going to that pub for over thirty years! How could you get lost?' Leaning close to his wife, so that the policeman can't hear him, Stanley whispers, 'I wasn't lost. I was just too tired to walk home!'

As we grow older, our bodies get shorter and our anecdotes longer.

ROBERT QUILLEN

Time wounds all heels.

Dorothy Parker

....

In a man's middle years there is scarcely a part of the body he would hesitate to turn over to the proper authorities.

E. B. White

....

Wrinkled was not one of the things I wanted to be when I grew up.

Robert Frost

A woman walks into a bar and orders a Scotch and two drops of water, 'It's my sixtieth birthday today,' she explains. The barman says, 'Well, since it's your birthday I'll buy you a drink.' As the woman finishes her drink a woman to her right says, 'I guess I should buy you a drink too.' The birthday girl says, 'All right. I'll have a Scotch and two drops of water.' As she finishes her drink, the man to her left says, 'Since I'm the only one that hasn't bought you a drink I guess I might as well buy you one too.' The woman says, 'OK, well make it another Scotch with two drops of water.' As the bartender gives her the drink he says, 'Madam, I'm dying of curiosity. Why the Scotch and only two drops of water?' The woman replies, 'Well, when you're my age, you realise that you can hold your liquor but you certainly can't hold your water!'

HAIR-UM
SCARE 'EM

I love bald men. Just because
you've lost your fuzz don't mean
you ain't a peach.

Dolly Parton

A man consults his friend about his increasing hair loss: 'I'm having to find more and more extravagant ways of combing my hair to make it look as if I have any left,' says one man. 'I know what you mean,' says a similarly balding man. 'I've seen men downcomb, up-comb and cross-comb. The thing is, you get to a stage where you only have three options left: parted, not parted and *de*parted.'

....

It's great to have a grey hair. Ask anyone who's bald.

Rodney Dangerfield

A balding gent walks into a barber shop and says, 'I'd like a haircut, please.' The hairdresser replies, 'Certainly, sir; which one?'

There is more felicity on the far side of baldness than young men can possibly imagine.

Logan Pearsall Smith

....

Two ladies in their sixties are discussing an upcoming dance at their country club. 'I've been told that the dress code is to wear something that matches our husband's hair, so I'll be wearing my black, silky dress with the silvery flecks!' says Mrs Smith with a chortle. 'Oh my goodness,' says Mrs Jones, thinking of her husband's bare noggin, 'I'd better not go in that case; I don't want to reveal *that* much!'

....

The whiter my hair becomes, the more ready people are to believe what I say.

Bertrand Russell

There is only one
cure for grey hair.
It was invented by a
Frenchman. It is called
the guillotine.

P. G. WODEHOUSE

A man whose hair has long since departed the top of his head sits down in the barber's chair, feeling despondent. He begins telling the barber about his bad experience at the hair transplant clinic: 'I thought, if it's good enough for Elton then it's good enough for me, but I couldn't stand the pain.' The man then brightens up when he comes up with a wager for the barber: 'If you can make my hair look like yours without causing me any discomfort, I'll pay you a thousand pounds.' The barber thinks about this for a moment, picks up his clippers and shaves his own head completely bare. 'That'll be one thousand pounds please, sir.'

....

I have a better head of hair than Rick Perry; it's just not in a place I can show you.

Kinky Friedman

My daughter teases me once in a while saying, 'Remember when you used to be my mother and you had black hair?'

Loni Anderson

....

They talk about the economy this year... my hairline is in recession, my waistline is in inflation. Altogether, I'm in a depression.

Rick Majerus

....

A hair in the head is worth two in the brush.

William Hazlitt

THE SOUNDS OF SILENCE

He needs to read lips.
I don't mind him reading lips,
but he uses one of those
yellow highlighters.

*Brian Kiley on his grandfather's
hearing problems*

A man goes to his doctor and says, 'I don't think my wife's hearing is as good as it used to be. What should I do?' The doctor replies, 'Try this test to find out for sure. When your wife is in the kitchen doing dishes, stand fifteen feet behind her and ask her a question, if she doesn't respond keep moving closer, asking the question until she hears you.' The man goes home and sees his wife preparing dinner. He stands fifteen feet behind her and says, 'What's for dinner, honey?' He gets no response, so he moves to ten feet behind her and asks again. Still no response, so he moves to five feet. Again, no answer. Finally he stands directly behind her and says, 'Honey, what's for supper?' She replies, 'For the fourth time, I SAID CHICKEN!'

Gloria and her lifelong friends Sally and Janice are discussing their increasing memory loss over a cup of tea: 'I think I must be getting old,' confides Sally. 'I sometimes find myself at the foot of the stairs, and I can't remember if I was going up to get something or coming back down.'
'I know what you mean,' says Janice. 'The other day I was in front of the fridge and I couldn't remember if I was taking something out, or if I had just put something in.' Gloria sits up and reaches for a biscuit. 'Well,' she says, 'I haven't had any problems like that so far, knock on wood', rapping three times on the table. Suddenly, looking a little startled, she stands up. 'Excuse me,' she says, 'Was that someone knocking at the door?'

An ageing gentleman is on the bus home from town, telling his friend about his new hearing aid: 'I've had hearing problems for years, as you know, so I thought it was about time I treated myself to a top-of-the-range hearing aid,' he says, pointing to the neat device in his ear. He continues, 'Eight hundred pounds it cost me... but it's worth it, it's absolutely perfect; I can hear the birds singing in the trees!'
'What kind is it?' his friend asks, looking suitably impressed. 'Oh, er... twelve thirty,' the man replies.

Two young boys are spending the night at their grandparents' house. At bedtime, the two boys kneel beside their beds to say their prayers. The youngest one begins praying at the top of his lungs: 'I PRAY FOR A BICYCLE… I PRAY FOR A NEW COMPUTER… I PRAY FOR A NEW DVD PLAYER…' His older brother leans over, nudges him and says, 'Why are you shouting your prayers? God isn't deaf.' To which the little brother replies, 'No, but grandma is!'

. . . .

One of the best hearing aids a man can have is an attentive wife.

Groucho Marx

An ageing man decides it's time he invested in a hearing aid, but he feels a little reluctant to spend lots of money. While investigating his options at the local hearing centre, the man asks, 'What price do your hearing aids start at?' To which the assistant replies, 'Our entry-level model is one hundred pounds, and our top of the line is five hundred.' The man considers this and still thinks the price is too much. 'Is there absolutely nothing cheaper?' he asks. 'Well,' the assistant says, 'I shouldn't really tell you this, but we do have some recovered models we could let you have for a small charge.' At this the man requests to see the cut-price model. 'You simply put this earpiece in and attach the wire to the inside of your pocket.' 'It seems a bit basic,' the man says, 'How does it work?'

'Well,' the assistant replies, 'for twenty pounds it doesn't work; but when people see you wearing it they'll start shouting at you anyway!'

Since I came to the White House, I got two hearing aids, a colon operation... and I was shot. The damn thing is I've never felt better in my life.

Ronald Reagan

....

Three old friends are out for an amble: 'Windy today, isn't it?' Geoff says. 'No,' Cyril says, 'it's Thursday!' Jim says, 'So am I. Let's go and get a pint.'

....

By deafness one gains in one respect more than one loses; one misses more nonsense than sense.

Horace Walpole

A senior lady is driving along the motorway, being careful to adhere to the speed limit and keep a safe distance from other cars. After a while she can see that a police car is behind her in the same lane. Feeling slightly self-conscious, she checks her speed and sees that she is well within the limit. However, the policeman continues to follow her and after a while she notices he's switched his flashing lights on. The lady decides to pull over. The policeman walks up to her window and begins speaking. As he does this, the lady points to her ear and shakes her head, indicating that she is deaf. The policeman smiles and knowing sign language, signs back, 'That's no problem, madam. I'm here to tell you that your horn is stuck!'

....

I would write plays for my grandmother, who was stone deaf, my mother and the dog; that was our audience.

Jayne Meadows

An elderly man decides that it has become necessary to invest in a hearing aid, and so visits a specialist, who gives him a device that restores his hearing completely. After a month, the man goes back for a check-up: 'Your hearing is perfect,' the specialist says, 'your family must be really pleased that you can hear again.' To which the man replies, 'Well, I haven't actually told my family yet. I've just been sitting around and listening to their conversations… and considering what they've been saying about me I can see I've got some big changes to make to my will!'

SIGHT, FOR SORE EYES

The easiest way to diminish the appearance of wrinkles is to keep your glasses off when you look in the mirror.

Joan Rivers

David and Paula, a couple in their late sixties, are getting ready for bed. Paula is undressing in front of her full-length mirror, taking a long, hard look at herself.

'You know, David,' she comments, 'I stare into this mirror and I see an ancient creature. My face has more crows feet than a bird sanctuary, my boobs have gone south, my bingo wings are big enough for me to take off and my bum is starting to look like a hundred-year-old saddle bag. Darling, please tell me just one positive thing about my body so I can feel better about myself.'

David studies Paula critically for a moment and then says in a soft, thoughtful voice, 'Well, dear, there is at least one thing that's in good nick – there is absolutely nothing wrong with your eyesight!'

....

I was walking down the street wearing glasses when the prescription ran out.

Steven Wright

My face in the mirror isn't wrinkled or drawn. My house isn't dirty. The cobwebs are gone. My garden looks lovely and so does my lawn. I think I might never put my glasses back on.

Anonymous

....

I don't read anything any more. I don't have the eyesight... I think I've read everything that's worth reading.

John Gould

I am getting to an age when I can only enjoy the last sport left. It is called hunting for your spectacles.

Edward Grey

Jack, a senior man, is giving his testimony in court. The defence lawyer asks Jack, 'Did you see my client commit this burglary?'

'Yes,' says Jack, 'I have no doubt it was him.' The lawyer, pressing Jack further, asks again: 'Now, Jack, this happened at night. Can you be entirely sure that it was my client you saw?'

'Yes,' says Jack, 'I saw him as plain as day.' Then the lawyer asks, 'Jack, with all due respect, at your age a man's eyesight isn't all that it used to be. Just how far can you see at night?' Jack says, 'Well, I can see the moon, how far is that?'

....

The grey-framed spectacles magnified the grey hazel eyes, but there was no greyness in the mind.

John Gunther

One day, Harry, a sporty man in his sixties, arrives home from an afternoon of golf, feeling depressed. 'I've decided I'm giving up golf. My eyesight has become so bad that once I've hit the ball, I can't see where it went.' His wife consoles him, makes him a nice cup of tea and says, 'Why don't you take our Arthur along next weekend and give it one more try?' 'That's no good,' sighs Harry. Your brother's ten years older than I am. He can't help.' 'He may be a bit older than you,' says the wife, 'but his eyesight has never been better.' So the next weekend, Harry heads off to the golf course with his brother-in-law. He tees up, makes his shot and looks down the fairway, squinting. He turns to his brother-in-law and asks, 'Did you see the ball?' 'Of course!' replies Arthur. 'I have perfect eyesight.' 'Right – where did it go?' asks Harry. 'Oh, er, sorry… I don't remember.'

If you ever find happiness by hunting for it, you will find it, as the old woman did her lost spectacles, safe on her own nose all the time.

JOSH BILLINGS

A senior woman pays a visit to her local pharmacy to complain about a product she's been using regularly. 'I've been applying this every day for a month and it's just not working,' the woman says, presenting the tube to the pharmacist. The pharmacist takes the product and examines it. 'Well,' the pharmacist says, 'to my knowledge this is a very effective and reliable treatment.' 'I've been brushing with it twice a day,' the woman insists, 'once in the morning and once at night, and I can honestly say it has done me no good.' 'Well madam, there shouldn't really be any need to use a brush – haemorrhoid cream can be applied quite easily without one,' says the pharmacist, looking slightly alarmed. 'Ah…' the woman replies, 'I see. Could you do me a favour and check your records? I think I might be due for an eye examination.'

BITING
BACK

I don't have false teeth. Do you
think I'd buy teeth like these?

Carol Burnett

A senior couple are enjoying a meal at a fine restaurant when all of a sudden the old man sneezes: 'I'm so proud of you,' his wife says, 'You've finally learned to put your hand in front of your mouth!' 'Of course I have,' her husband replies crossly, 'How the hell else am I going to catch my teeth?'

. . . .

A boy visits his grandma with his mate. While the boy is talking to his grandma in the kitchen, his friend helps himself to some peanuts from a bowl. When it's time to go his friend calls out: 'Thanks for the peanuts!' 'That's all right,' the grandma replies. 'Since I lost my dentures I can only suck the chocolate off them!'

Laughter doesn't require teeth.
Bill Newton

A care home nurse brings her six-year-old daughter to work one day to have a look around. The little girl is fascinated by all the paraphernalia, such as the walkers, wheelchairs and gripping devices. They pay one lady a special visit, she has just got up and is yet to put her teeth in. The little girl's eyes widen in shock on seeing the full set of false teeth floating in a glass. She turns to her mum and whispers, 'The tooth fairy will never believe this!'

....

I told my dentist my teeth are going yellow. He told me to wear a brown tie.

Rodney Dangerfield

What's one thing that an old person can do that a younger person can't? Sing aloud whilst brushing their teeth!

. . . .

An old couple are sitting down at a table in a restaurant, waiting for their food to arrive. The waiter sets down their meals and notices a short while later that they are meticulously splitting the food between the two of them. Fair enough, he thinks, but then he notices that the wife is just sitting there while the husband is busily tucking in. He then asks them if there's any problem with the food. 'Oh, no,' the old man says, 'it's just that after fifty years of marriage we always split everything down the middle.' Still a little confused, the waiter then asks the lady if she's going to eat, and she replies, 'Not yet. You see, it's *his* turn with the teeth!'

After eating his dinner, an old man coughs violently, sending his false teeth flying across the room. 'Oh dear,' he says, 'they're ruined… smashed to bits. There's no way I can afford another set.'
'Don't worry, Dad,' says his son, 'I'll get a pair from my pal at work. Just give me what's left of your set so I can give him an idea of the size.' The next day the son comes back with the teeth, which fit perfectly. 'This is wonderful, son,' says the man. 'Your friend must be a very good dentist.'
'Oh,' says the son, 'he's not a dentist, he's an undertaker.'

....

We idolised the Beatles [and] the Rolling Stones, who in those days still had many of their original teeth.

Dave Barry

While watching a movie at the cinema, an elderly man begins rummaging around at the feet of the people sitting next to him. Becoming slightly annoyed at him, the lady in the neighbouring seat whispers crossly, 'Just what is it that you're doing down there?' 'I've lost a toffee,' the old man replies. 'You're going through all that bother just for a toffee?' the woman asks. 'Yes,' says the old man, 'you see, my teeth are in it.'

Two ladies, fiercely competitive in their latter years, are attending a dinner at their favourite country club. 'Well, Margaret,' one says, 'you're looking absolutely splendid tonight. And what's this?' she asks, noticing her necklace, 'Real pearls, I suppose?'
'Why yes, dear,' Margaret replies. '
Of course,' the other retorts, 'in order to tell for sure, I'd have to bite them, what?'
'I'd be perfectly happy for you to do that, dear,' Margaret says, 'except, you'd need real teeth for that, wouldn't you?'

....

She had so many gold teeth... she used to have to sleep with her head in a safe.

W. C. Fields

MEDICATION'S
WHATCHA
NEED

Every time I hear it, I think I'm supposed to put my breast in an envelope and send it to someone.

Jan King on the word 'mammogram'

A hospital bed is a parked taxi with the meter running.

Groucho Marx

....

A man in his sixties with a much younger wife decides to try Viagra so that he can keep up with her demands in the bedroom. They go to pick up his Viagra prescription, but the man baulks upon seeing the £30-per-pill price. His wife, on the other hand, looks indifferent… 'I don't know,' she says, 'thirty pounds a year isn't so bad.'

....

I'm taking Viagra and drinking prune juice – I don't know if I'm coming or going.

Rodney Dangerfield

An ageing woman goes to her doctor to see what he can recommend for her troublesome constipation. 'It's terrible,' she says to the doctor. 'I haven't had a bowel movement in more than a week.'
'I see. Have you done anything about it?' asks the doctor. 'Oh, yes,' she replies, 'I sit in the bathroom for a good half an hour in the morning and then again at night.'
'No,' the doctor says, 'I mean do you take anything?'
'Of course I do,' she answers, 'I take the crossword book.'

....

A senior man is recovering from surgery when a nurse asks him how he is feeling. 'I'm OK but I didn't like the four-letter-word the doctor used in surgery,' he replies. 'What did he say?' asks the nurse, looking concerned.
'OOPS!' He exclaims.

A man comes home from work and notices his father has hidden himself behind the sofa. 'What's the problem?' he asks his dad. 'Are the children getting a bit too rowdy today?' The old man shakes his head and reaches into his trouser pocket for his prescription and points to the small print, 'Read the label,' he says, 'Take two pills a day. KEEP AWAY FROM CHILDREN.'

A retired gentleman goes to the doctor and tells him that he hasn't been feeling well. The doctor examines him, leaves the room and comes back with three different bottles of pills. The doctor says, 'Take the green pill with a big glass of water when you get up. Take the blue pill with a big glass of water after lunch. Then just before going to bed, take the red pill with another big glass of water.' Startled to be put on so much medicine, the elderly man stammers, 'My goodness, exactly what's my problem?' The doctor says, 'You're not drinking enough water.'

. . . .

A senior man is nervously awaiting the results of his medical when the doctor returns with his results. 'Well, doctor,' he says, 'how do I stand?' 'To be honest,' the doctor replies, 'that's what's puzzling me.'

Now I'm getting older I don't need to do drugs any more. I can get the same effect just by standing up real fast.

JONATHAN KATZ

An old man goes to the pharmacy for some cough syrup. The assistant can't find any so he recommends a strong laxative. The old man asks, 'How will a laxative help my congestion?' 'It won't,' replies the assistant, 'but you'll be too scared to cough.'

....

A woman is waiting at the pharmacy for her HRT prescription. As the pharmacist hands over her medicine, he makes a point of explaining the dosage directions: 'Now, Mrs Smith, it's important that you take no more than one tablet every four hours.' To which Mrs Smith replies, 'There'll be no problems there, I can assure you. It usually takes me at least two hours to find the bottle, and another two to get the damn lid off!'

STAYIN' ALIVE

I exercise every morning without fail. One eyelid goes up and the other follows.

Pete Postlethwaite

Muscles come and go; flab lasts.
Bill Vaughan

....

A gentleman is telling his friend about his new exercise regime: 'I think I'm a little old for all this gym stuff, but I'm building up some equipment at home. I got one of those Ab Roller contraptions recently. Thing is, I've been rolling it up and down my stomach for the past six weeks, and all I've got to show for it is this unsightly red line down my middle!'

....

It is better to wear out than to rust out.
Richard Cumberland

The best, the most exquisite automobile is a walking stick; and one of the finest things in life is going on a journey with it.

Robert Coates Holliday

....

'My doctor told me if I took up jogging it could add ten years to my life,' a middle-aged man was telling his friend. 'He was absolutely right – I now feel ten years older.'

....

The dead centre of middle age... occurs when you are too young to take up golf and too old to rush to the net.

Franklin Adams

A determined lady of a certain age is telling a friend about her new aerobics class: 'I felt as if I was completely out of shape, so I just went for it. I stretched, twisted, jumped up and down and wiggled... Of course, by the time I'd got my leotard on, the class had finished.'

A man is standing on the bathroom scales desperately sucking his stomach in. 'That's not going to help,' says his wife. 'Yes it will,' replies the man. 'It's the only way I can see the numbers.'

....

A health specialist is giving a talk on wellbeing to an over-fifties club in the local village hall. 'The best way to start the day is to do five minutes of light exercise, and five minutes of deep breathing,' says the specialist. 'Then I take a hot shower, and feel rosy all over.' There are nods of agreement from the group until one wisecrack at the back pipes up: 'Tell us more about Rosie!'

Health nuts are going to feel
stupid someday, lying in hospitals
dying of nothing.

Redd Foxx

....

How pleasant is the day when we give up
striving to be young – or slender.

William James

....

My doctor told me to do something that
puts me out of breath, so I've taken up
smoking again.

Jo Brand

It's no longer a question of staying healthy. It's a question of finding a sickness you like.

Jackie Mason

....

An older woman goes to a leisure centre and asks if she can join a gym class. 'I'm not sure if that's a good idea,' says the instructor. 'How flexible are you?' 'Oh, very,' replies the woman. 'But I can't make Tuesdays.'

HOLDING BACK THE YEARS

I don't plan to grow old gracefully. I plan to have facelifts until my ears meet.

Rita Rudner

A sixty-year-old woman decides it's high time she had a facelift, so she goes for a consultation at a smart clinic. 'We have a new procedure,' the surgeon explains. 'We put a small screw in the top of your head, so that any time you see wrinkles reappearing, you simply turn the screw to tighten and lift the skin.' She thinks this sounds marvellous and signs up to the procedure that very day. However, the woman soon starts to experience problems and returns a few months later to give the surgeon a piece of her mind, 'This is the biggest mistake I've ever made! Just look at these terrible bags under my eyes!'

'Madam,' the surgeon replies, 'those are not bags, those are your breasts.'

....

There is still no cure for the common birthday.

John Glenn

I'm sixty-three now, but that's just seventeen Celsius.

George Carlin

....

Age is not a particularly interesting subject. Anyone can get old. All you have to do is live long enough.

Groucho Marx

....

Looking fifty is great – if you're sixty.

Joan Rivers

I've found the secret of eternal youth.
I lie about my age.

Bob Hope

....

Beautiful young people are accidents
of nature, but beautiful old people are
works of art.

Eleanor Roosevelt

....

I refuse to admit I'm more than
fifty-two, even if that does make my
sons illegitimate.

Nancy Astor

A traffic policeman stops a female motorist for speeding. 'Madam,' he begins, 'I'm sure you know exactly why I stopped you. As you came down the street I had you at sixty-five, minimum.'

'Outrageous!' the woman replies. 'I'm not a day over fifty-five. And besides, there's no way you could have made an accurate estimate – I was driving far too fast for that.'

In dog years, I'm dead.

Anonymous

....

A woman's always younger than a man of equal years.

Elizabeth Barrett Browning

....

I do wish I could tell you my age but it's impossible. It keeps changing all the time.

Greer Garson

A lady goes into a cosmetics store and asks for a new anti-ageing cream she has seen on TV. She spends the next month applying it day and night, but isn't sure if it's working or not. She decides to ask her husband: 'Darling, be honest, what age would you say I am?'

'Well,' he says, 'judging from your skin, I would say twenty; your hair, eighteen; your body, twenty-five.'

'Oh! You say all the right things,' she cries, covering him in kisses. 'Hang on,' the husband says, 'you didn't give me a chance to add them up!'

There are three ages of man – youth, age, and, 'You're looking wonderful.'

Francis Spellman

....

No man is ever old enough to know better.

Holbrook Jackson

....

No woman should ever be quite accurate about her age. It looks so calculating.

Oscar Wilde

Jewellery takes people's minds off your wrinkles.

Sonja Henie

....

A man who correctly guesses a woman's age may be smart, but he's not very bright.

Lucille Ball

....

Men become much more attractive when they start looking older. But it doesn't do much for women, though we do have an advantage: make-up.

Bette Davis

··

*I have never known
a person to live to be
one hundred and
be remarkable for
anything else.*

JOSH BILLINGS

··

Old age is fifteen years older than I am.

Oliver Wendell Holmes

....

Time and tide wait for no man, but time always stands still for a woman of thirty.

Robert Frost

....

As a graduate of the Zsa Zsa Gabor School of creative mathematics, I honestly do not know how old I am.

Erma Bombeck

Age to women is like Kryptonite to Superman.

Kathy Lette

Please don't retouch my wrinkles. It took me so long to earn them.

Anna Magnani

....

I don't believe in ageing. I believe in forever altering one's aspect to the sun.

Virginia Woolf

....

Time may be a great healer, but it's a lousy beautician.

Anonymous

LOVE ME TENDER

An archaeologist is the best husband any woman can have: the older she gets, the more interested he is in her.

Agatha Christie

After thirty years of marriage, a man looks at his wife one day and says, 'You know, thirty years ago we lived in a cheap apartment, drove a rusty old car and made do with a tiny twelve-inch TV set. Yet, every night I got to sleep with a hot twenty-five-year-old blonde. Now,' he continues, 'we have a beautiful house, an expensive car, a big flat-screen TV, but I have to sleep with a fifty-five-year-old woman. It doesn't seem fair.'

'Well,' she snaps, 'why don't you go out and get yourself a hot twenty-five-year-old blonde? Then, once the divorce papers have gone through, you will be living in a cheap apartment, driving a rusty old car and watching a tiny twelve-inch TV set.'

....

A wedding anniversary is the celebration of love, trust, partnership, tolerance and tenacity. The order varies for any given year.

Paul Sweeney

A senior couple are sitting together watching television. During an advert showing a young, passionate couple the husband turns to his wife and asks, 'Whatever happened to our sexual relations?' After a long, thoughtful silence, the wife replies, 'You know, I'm not sure. Gordon completely forgot your birthday and we didn't even get a Christmas card from your sister this year!'

. . . .

An older couple are planning their wedding, and before the big day they have a long conversation about how their marriage might work. They discuss the usual things like finances, living arrangements and so on. After some hesitation, the old man broaches the subject of sex. 'How do you feel about sex?' he asks hopefully. 'Well, I have to admit, at my age I like it infrequently,' she replies. The old man is silent for a moment and then asks, 'Sorry – was that one word or two?'

Two senior newly-weds are trying to get things started in the love-making department but they're not getting anywhere. 'You'll have to do something,' says the man. 'Like what?' asks his wife. 'You know,' he says, 'like moaning and stuff.' Thinking this is a reasonable idea, the woman begins: 'Would you look at the state of those curtains, they're hideous! And the dust on that dressing table! Didn't your mother teach you how to fold your trousers properly?'

I'd marry again if I found a man who had fifteen million dollars, would sign over half to me, and guarantee that he'd be dead within a year.

Bette Davis

....

Two men are pushing their trolleys around a hardware store when they collide. The older man says to the younger one, 'Sorry about that. I'm a little preoccupied – I can't find my wife, you see.' The young man says, 'That's OK. I'm looking for my wife too, actually. I can't find her and I'm getting a little desperate.'

'Well,' says the old man, 'two heads are better than one – let's help each other. What does your wife look like?'

'Well, she's twenty-four years old; blonde hair; blue eyes; she's wearing a short blue skirt… What does your wife look like?' 'Never mind,' the old man says excitedly, 'let's look for yours first!'

Never feel remorse for what you have thought about your wife; she has thought much worse things about you.

Jean Rostand

....

A husband and wife are having a bitter quarrel on the day of their ruby wedding anniversary. The husband yells, 'When you die, I'm getting you a headstone that reads, "Here Lies My Wife – Cold as Ever".' 'Well,' the wife replies, 'When you die, I'm getting you a headstone that reads, "Here Lies My Husband – Stiff at Last".'

....

The concept of two people living together for twenty-five years without a serious dispute suggests a lack of spirit only to be admired in sheep.

A. P. Herbert

I have learned that only two things are necessary to keep one's wife happy. First, let her think she's having her own way. And second, let her have it.

LYNDON B. JOHNSON

It used to be wine, women and song. Now, it's beer, the old lady and TV!

Anonymous

....

An old professor visits his doctor for a routine check-up and everything seems fine. The doctor proceeds to ask him about his sex life. 'Well,' the professor drawls, 'not bad at all, to be honest. The wife isn't all that interested any more, so I just cruise around. In the past week I have been able to pick up and bed at least three girls, none of whom were over thirty years old.'

'My goodness, and at your age too!' the doctor says with surprise. 'I hope you at least took some precautions.'

'Yep. I may be old, but I'm not senile yet. I gave them all a fake name.'

Tony is trying to persuade his wife, Alison, to go up in a plane at the local air show: 'But the ride is fifty pounds, and fifty pounds is fifty pounds,' argues Alison. Luckily for Tony, a pilot is walking past and overhears their argument. He walks up to them and says, 'Listen, folks, I'll make you a deal. I'll take you both up for a ride. If you can stay quiet for the entire ride I won't charge you, but if you say one word it's fifty pounds!' The couple agree to his terms and up they go. The pilot performs all kinds of rolls, twists and dives, and the couple remain absolutely silent. After a perfect landing, the pilot turns round to Tony and says, 'I'm impressed. I did everything I could think of to get you to yell out, but you didn't.' To which Tony replies, 'Well, I was going to say something when Alison fell out, but, after all, fifty pounds is fifty pounds!'

RELIGHT MY FIRE

At my age I'm envious of a stiff wind.

Rodney Dangerfield

Two elderly men are talking about Viagra. One has never heard of it and asks the other what it is for. 'It's the greatest invention ever,' he says. 'It makes you feel like a man of thirty.'
'Can you get it over the counter?'
'Probably – if you took four.'

. . . .

A sixty-year-old man goes to the doctor's and says: 'Doc, my sex drive is too high – I want it lowered.' The doctor can't believe what he is hearing. 'You're sixty and you want your sex drive lowered?' 'That's right,' says the man pointing to his head. 'It's all up here. I want it lowered.'

. . . .

I once saw my grandparents have sex, and that's why I don't eat raisins.

Zach Galifianakis

Everything that goes up must come down. But there comes a time when not everything that's down can come up.

George Burns

....

An old man goes to church to make a confession. 'Father,' he begins, 'I'm sixty-two years old. I've been married for forty years. Until recently I had been faithful to my wife, but yesterday I was intimate with an eighteen-year-old model.' The priest replies, 'I see. And when was your last confession?' The old man says, 'Actually, I've never been to confession. I'm Jewish.'
'So, why are you telling me about this young girl?' asks the priest. 'I'm not just telling you,' says the old man excitedly, 'I'm telling everybody!'

An old lady is feeling lonely living on her own, so she decides to buy a pet to keep her company. At the pet shop she stops to take a closer look at a frog, and to her surprise he whispers, 'Take me home and you won't be sorry.' So the old lady picks him up and gets into her car. Driving down the road the frog whispers again to her, 'Kiss me and you won't be sorry.' The old lady thinks about this and says, 'Well, why not?' So she stops the car and stoops down to kiss the frog. All of a sudden, in a blaze of fireworks and coloured smoke, the frog transforms into a handsome young man. The young man kisses the old lady in return, and you know what the old lady turned into? The first B&B she could find!

A man, getting on a bit, begins to find that he is unable to perform sexually. After trying everything conventional medicine has to offer, he decides to take a chance on a medicine man, who gives him a vial of blue liquid. 'This is powerful stuff,' the medicine man says. 'All you have to do is say "one-two-three", and you'll instantly rise to the occasion. When your partner is completely satisfied, all she has to say is "one-two-three-four", and the liquid will wear off.' The old gent rushes home, anxious to try out this new wonder potion. That night, he drinks the liquid, cuddles up to his wife and says 'one- two-three', and suddenly he's ready for action, just as the medicine man promised. Just then, his wife turns to him and asks, 'What did you say "one-two-three" for?'

....

When did my wild oats turn into shredded wheat?

Anonymous

A terrible thing happened to me last night again – nothing.

Phyllis Diller

....

Two senior singles, Jack and Audrey, meet at a dance one evening, and after several weeks of going for coffees, decide to go out for dinner on a proper date. They have a lovely evening dining at the most romantic restaurant in town, after which they go to his place for a nightcap. Things continue along a natural course and, age being no inhibitor, Audrey soon joins Jack for a bit of rough and tumble. Afterwards, as they both lie smiling, they quietly ponder this special moment: Jack thinks to himself: 'If I'd known she was a virgin, I'd have been gentler.' Audrey thinks: 'If I'd known he could still do it, I'd have taken my tights off.'

I can still enjoy sex at seventy-four. I live at seventy-five, so it's no distance.

Bob Monkhouse

....

A man is surprised to find his elderly father sitting on his deck chair in the garden, with no trousers on. 'What on earth are you doing sitting out here with no trousers on?' he asks. The old man looks at him slyly and says, 'Well, last week I sat out here with no shirt on and I got a stiff neck. This was your mother's idea!'

....

Continental people have sex lives; the English have hot-water bottles.

George Mikes

Two senior men are discussing the ups and downs of their sex lives: 'Did you know,' one says, 'that scientists have recently developed a soluble form of Viagra? I dropped one into my cuppa the other day.'

'Did it work?' the other man asks. 'Well,' the first man says, 'it didn't enhance my sexual performance, but it did stop my biscuit going soft!'

A noted sex therapist comes to the conclusion that people often lie about the frequency of their encounters, so he devises a test to tell how often someone has sex. To prove his theory, he fills an auditorium with people, and asks each person in turn to smile. Using the size of the person's smile, the therapist is able to guess accurately until he comes to the last man in line, an elderly gentleman, who is grinning from ear to ear. 'Twice a day,' the therapist guesses. But the therapist is surprised when the man says no. 'Once a day, then?' Again the answer is no. 'Twice a week?' 'No.' 'Twice a month?' 'No.' The man finally says yes when the therapist asks 'Once a year?' Annoyed that his theory has been disproved, the therapist snaps, 'Then what on earth are you so happy about?' The gent answers, 'Tonight's the night!'

....

My best birth control now is to leave the lights on.

Joan Rivers

I only take Viagra when I'm with more than one woman.

Jack Nicholson

....

An old man goes to the doctor for his annual check-up. The doctor listens to his heart and pronounces: 'I'm afraid you have a serious heart murmur. Do you smoke at all?' The man says no. 'Do you drink to excess?' Again, the man says no. 'Do you still have a sex life?' the doctor asks. 'Yes,' the man replies. 'Well, I'm sorry to have to tell you,' the doctor says, 'but with this heart murmur, you'll have to give up half of your sex life.' Looking a bit perplexed, the old man answers, 'Which half – the looking or the thinking?'

OLD-FASHIONED ROMANCE

You know you're over the hill when the only whistles you get are from the tea kettle.

Raquel Welch

I'll see a beautiful girl walking up to me...
I can't believe my good luck. But then
she'll say, 'Where's your son?' or
'My mother loves you.'

James Caan

. . . .

A mature man decides to throw caution to the
wind and approach a young female library clerk
he has taken a shine to. He goes up to the counter
and with a sly wink says, 'You know, some people
say that when a man reaches a certain maturity he
becomes attractive even to someone half his age...
have you ever heard that?'
'Yes,' she says, smiling brightly, 'as a matter of fact I
have. Fictional Romance, aisle four.'

One of the best parts of growing older? You can flirt all you like since you've become harmless.

Liz Smith

Reg, a sixty-three-year-old postman, has worked hard all his life, never finding the time to get married. But one day a beautiful nineteen-year-old girl walks into his office and it is love at first sight. Within a month, Reg and Rachel get married and go to Butlins for their honeymoon. 'So how was it?' asks Bill, one of Reg's colleagues back at the post office. 'Oh, just beautiful,' replies a starry-eyed Reg. 'The cream teas, the karaoke… and we made love almost every night, we –'

'Just a minute,' interrupts Bill. 'At your age, forgive me for asking, you made love almost every night?'

'Oh yes,' says Reg, 'we almost made love Saturday, we almost made love Sunday…'

Old age is when a guy keeps turning off lights for economical rather than romantic reasons.

Anonymous

A senior couple are in a romantic mood. While the pair are wrapped up in bed the wife says, 'I remember when you used to kiss me every chance you could get.' So the husband leans over and gives her a little peck on the cheek. Then she says, 'I also remember how you used to hold my hand all the time.' So he reaches over and gently squeezes her hand. 'I can also remember when you used to nibble on my ear,' the wife says. The husband sighs, stands up, and starts to make his way out of the room. 'Where are you going?' asks the wife. 'To find my teeth,' says the husband.

....

An ageing woman is telling her daughter about a date she has been on with a retired gentleman that she recently met. 'Can you believe I had to slap his face three times?' she says. 'What do you mean,' the daughter asks, 'did he get a little frisky?' 'Oh, no!' her mother explains, 'I had to slap him three times to keep the old bugger awake!'

Love is not a matter of counting the years... but making the years count.

Michelle Amand

....

A widow and widower have been dating for about two years. After a happy courtship, the man decides to ask for the lady's hand in marriage. When he asks her, the lady is overjoyed and immediately says yes. The next morning, he struggles to remember what her answer had been! He thinks to himself: 'Was she happy when I asked? I think so... but she did look at me funny.' After about an hour of trying to remember to no avail, he decides to give her a call. Embarrassed, he admits that he can't remember her answer to the marriage proposal. 'Oh,' she says, 'I'm so glad you called. You see, I remembered saying yes to someone, but I couldn't remember who I said it to!'

Men always want to be a woman's first love. Women have a more subtle instinct: what they like is to be a man's last romance.

Oscar Wilde

....

To keep the heart unwrinkled, to be hopeful, kindly, cheerful, reverent that is to triumph over old age.

Thomas B. Aldrich

....

Food has taken the place of sex in my life... I've just had a mirror put over my kitchen table.

Rodney Dangerfield

A retired lady goes to visit her daughter and finds her naked, waiting for her husband Tim to return from work. The mother asks: 'What on earth are you doing with no clothes on?' To which the daughter replies shyly, 'Well, this is my "love dress" – I'm waiting for Tim to come home.' After the mother gets home, she decides to strip naked and surprise her husband. Upon arriving home, her husband asks, 'Dear, what are you doing with no clothes on?' With a smile she says, 'This is my "love dress" of course!' To which he replies, 'Well dear, I suggest you go and iron it.'

. . . .

Two older women are watching their husbands from a bench as they wander through the park. 'Looks like your Edward still likes to chase the ladies,' one says, as she sees him greet a young girl he passes. 'It doesn't worry me,' the other says. 'Even if he could catch one he wouldn't be able to remember what he wanted them for!'

A couple of old chaps are taking a quiet stroll when they see a group of teenage girls. One says, 'You know, when I see pretty girls like that it makes me want to be thirty years older.' 'What?! Don't be daft,' says the other. You're sixty years old. If anything you should be wishing you were thirty years *younger*.' 'Maybe,' the other replies. 'But if I were thirty years older, I'd be past caring.'

A retired divorcee decides he needs a little romance in his life, and so goes out to try and find himself a girl. After trying his luck at several of the seniors' dances and bingo nights, one evening he decides to stop off at a local pub. As he's commiserating with a pint he notices a young, shy-looking woman in the corner smiling at him. He decides to throw caution to the wind and ask if she'd like some company, to which she replies, yes. The man can't believe his luck, and as the night progresses they seem to be getting on like a house on fire. As the pub is about to close, the woman invites him back to her place. They end up in the bedroom, when the man asks, 'So, did your mother tell you everything you need to know about spending the night with a man?'

'Oh, yes,' she replies. 'That's lucky,' the man says, 'because at my age you tend to forget these things!'

LAST
INNINGS

I intend to live forever,
or die trying.

Groucho Marx

He is alive, but only in the sense that he can't be legally buried.

Geoffrey Madan

....

A senior lady is at her husband's funeral. She tells her daughter that throughout their married life they had enjoyed physical relations each and every Sunday morning in time to the church bells. 'Maybe he was getting a bit old for that sort of thing,' says the daughter. 'Nonsense,' replies the old lady. 'If it hadn't been for that ice cream van, he'd still be alive today.'

....

When doctors and undertakers meet, they always wink at each other.

W. C. Fields

The idea is to die young as late as possible.

Ashley Montagu

....

George visits his solicitor to make a will. 'So what exactly do I do?' he asks. 'I'll just need you to answer a few questions, then you can leave it all to me,' says the solicitor. 'Well,' says George, 'I do thoroughly appreciate what you're doing for me, but I was hoping to leave at least some of it to my wife.'

....

How young can you die of old age?

Steven Wright

My grandmother was a very tough woman. She buried three husbands and two of them were just napping.

Rita Rudner

Three elderly gentlemen are talking about what their grandchildren might say about them after they've passed on. 'I would like my grandchildren to say, "He was successful in business",' declares the first man. 'I want them to say, "He was a loyal family man",' says the second. Turning to the third gent, the first gent asks, 'So what do you want them to say about you in fifty years?' 'Me?' the third man replies. 'I want them all to say, "He certainly looks good for his age"!'

. . . .

No one is so old as to think he cannot live one more year.

Marcus T. Cicero

I hope I never get so old I get religious.

Ingmar Bergman

....

I look at the obituary page. If my name is not on it, I get up.

Harry Hershfield on his morning routine

....

I don't think anyone should write their autobiography until after they're dead.

Samuel Goldwyn

DRIVING MISS DAISY

That's a good thing. He's getting old. He ran his entire last race with his left blinker on.

Jon Stewart on Mario Andretti's retirement from car racing

A group of ladies are chatting about their ailments over a cuppa. 'My arm is so weak I can hardly hold this teacup,' one complains. 'Yes, I know what you mean,' says another. 'My cataracts are so bad I can't see to pour the tea.'
'I can't turn my head because of the arthritis in my neck,' another friend says. 'My blood pressure pills make me feel faint.' 'I guess that's the price we pay for reaching our seventies,' one suggests. 'Well, it's not all bad... at least we're all still allowed to drive!'

....

If God wanted us to walk, he'd have given us pogo sticks instead of feet. Feet are made to fit car pedals.

Stirling Moss

The elderly don't drive that badly; they're just the only ones with time to do the speed limit.

Jason Love

A man is driving down the motorway when his mobile rings. It's his wife. 'Jack, drive carefully, I just heard on the news that there's a car going the wrong way on the motorway.'

'Tell me about it,' he replies. 'It's not just one, there are hundreds of them.'

. . . .

While on a car trip, an elderly couple stop at the services for lunch. After finishing their meal, the woman absentmindedly leaves her glasses on the table, but she doesn't miss them until they are well into their journey. 'I'm sorry, Jim,' the wife says, 'but I've left my glasses at the service station. We'll have to go back for them.' The man fusses and complains all the way back to the restaurant, cursing his wife under his breath. When they finally arrive at the restaurant, as the woman gets out of the car to retrieve her glasses, her husband says sheepishly, 'While you're in there, dear, you might as well get my hat, too.'

If you don't like the
way I drive, stay off
the sidewalk!

JOAN RIVERS

An old lady is walking back to her car after doing the weekly shop at the supermarket. As she nears her car, she is shocked to find four strange-looking men sitting in it. She drops her shopping and draws a handgun from her bag and screams, 'Get out of my car this instant you scoundrels. I've got a gun!' The four men jump out of the car and run as fast as they can out of the car park. After a few minutes of trying the key she realises that it doesn't fit… she gets out to see her own car parked five spaces down the row. Feeling overwhelmed with guilt, she drives to the nearest police station. As she's explaining her story to the sergeant at the station, he begins to giggle uncontrollably and points to the desk opposite, where four petrified men are telling another officer how they were carjacked half an hour ago by a crazed old lady with a bobble hat and a .44 Magnum!

As you get older you need to sleep more. My favourite time is on the motorway, during rush hour.

Bob Hope

....

It finally happened. I got the GPS lady so confused, she said, 'In one-quarter mile, make a legal stop and ask directions.'

Robert Brault

....

I saw a second-hand car last week that was so old it had bifocal headlights.

Edward Philips

?

··

PARTIAL
RECALL

··

Sometimes it's fun to sit in
your garden and try to remember
your dog's name.

Steve Martin

First you forget names... Next you forget to pull your zipper up and finally, you forget to pull it down.

George Burns

....

Two dear old friends of many years are playing cards, when one says: 'My friend, this is terrible, but can you remind me what your name is?' Her friend gives her a long, hard stare, then replies: 'How soon do you need to know?'

....

Three things happen when you get to my age. First your memory starts to go and I've forgotten the other two.

Denis Healey

It is lovely, when I forget all birthdays, including my own, to find that somebody remembers me.

Ellen Glasgow

....

A well-dressed, debonair man in his eighties enters a swanky cocktail bar and finds a seat next to a good-looking, younger woman in her mid-sixties, at the most. Trying to remember his best chat-up line, he says, 'So tell me, do I come here often?'

....

The advantage of a bad memory is that one enjoys several times the same good things for the first time.

Friedrich Nietzsche

Perhaps being old is having lighted rooms inside your head, and people in them, acting. People you know, yet can't quite name.

Philip Larkin

....

A senior lady calls 999 on her mobile phone to report that her car has been broken into. In a hysterical state, she describes the situation to the operator: 'They've stolen the steering wheel, the brake pedal and even the accelerator!' she cries. The operator tells her to keep calm, and that a police officer is on his way. A few minutes later, the officer reports back to the station. 'Disregard,' he says, 'She got in the back seat by mistake.'

....

I have a photographic memory. Unfortunately, it no longer offers same-day service.

Anonymous

Those who cannot remember the past will spend a lot of time looking for their cars in mall parking lots.

Jay Trachman

A retired couple go to dinner at the home of some old friends. After dinner, the two men get talking. One says, 'Last week we ate at a marvellous restaurant. I highly recommend it.' The second man says, 'Well, I'll take your word for it. What was it called?' The first man pauses, thinking intently, then says, 'What's the name of that flower you give to someone to be romantic, the one that is usually red that has thorns?'

'Oh, you mean a rose?' asks the second man. 'Yes, that's it,' says the first man. Then he calls into the kitchen, 'Rose, what's the name of that restaurant we went to last week?'

....

Old age puts more wrinkles in our minds than on our faces.

Michel de Montaigne

When it comes to staying young, a mind–lift beats a facelift any day.

MARTY BUCELLA

A travel agent looks up from his desk to see an older couple at the window, peering inside at the posters showing the glamorous destinations around the world. The agent, having reached his sales targets for the week and feeling a sudden wave of generosity come over him, decides to call the couple into the shop and says to them, 'I know that on your pension you could never hope to go on a luxury holiday, so I am sending you away at my expense – and I won't take no for an answer!' The couple are overjoyed, and within a week are on their way to an exotic, five-star resort. About a month later, the lady returns to the shop. 'And how did you like your holiday?' he asks eagerly. 'The flight was exciting and the room was lovely,' she says. 'I've come to thank you. But, one thing is still puzzling me. Who was that old guy I had to share the room with?'

A man goes to his friends' home for dinner. During the meal, he notices his friend addressing his wife with endearing nicknames, calling her 'honey', 'my love', 'sweetheart' and so on. While the wife is off in the kitchen, the man says to his friend, 'I think it's wonderful that after all these years you still love your wife enough to call her those pet names.' His friend hangs his head and replies, 'To tell you the truth, it's because I forgot her name about ten years ago.'

....

As you get older three things happen. The first is your memory goes, and I can't remember the other two...

Norman Wisdom

OLD FOLKS, AT HOME

As I get older, I just prefer to knit

Tracey Ullman

Two retired professors are sitting on the patio one fine evening, watching the sun set. The history professor asks the psychology professor, 'Have you read Marx?' To which the professor of psychology replies, 'Yes, and I think it's these blasted wicker chairs!'

....

Preparation for old age should begin not later than one's teens. A life which is empty of purpose until sixty-five will not suddenly become filled on retirement.

Dwight L. Moody

The first sign of maturity is the discovery that the volume knob also turns to the left.

Jerry M. Wright

When you're a young man, Macbeth is a character part. When you're older, it's a straight part.

Laurence Olivier

. . . .

I've got to watch myself these days. It's too exciting watching anyone else.

Bob Hope

. . . .

When men reach their sixties and retire they go to pieces. Women just go right on cooking.

Gail Sheehy

Getting old is a fascinating thing. The older you get, the older you want to get.

Keith Richards

....

At sixty-five, Jill decides she's ready to retire. At her leaving party at work her boss makes a speech: 'Well, Jill, there's no doubt that after you've left we'll find it hard to replace you... You could even say you are irreplaceable. Of course, that's mainly down to the fact that, for the past ten years, we're not entirely sure what it was you did around here!'

....

People are living longer than ever before, a phenomenon undoubtedly made necessary by the thirty-year mortgage.

Doug Larson

A man of sixty has
spent twenty years in
bed and over three years
in eating.

ARNOLD BENNETT

At his retirement presentation, Tom's boss decides to say a few words. 'We'd like to thank Tom for his many years of service to the company… I can say with absolute certainty that he's a man who, while at work, didn't know the meaning of "impossible task", who never took the words "lunch break" to heart, and who has shown professional contempt for the command "no". So, Tom, we've all clubbed together and bought you… a dictionary.'

....

Retirement at sixty-five is ridiculous. When I was sixty-five I still had pimples.

George Burns

I still have a full deck;
I just shuffle slower now.

Anonymous

THE GIFT OF GRANDKIDS

Grandchildren don't make a man feel old; it's the knowledge that he's married to a grandmother.

Agatha Christie

A young mother's three-year-old son opens a birthday gift from his grandmother, and is delighted to discover that it's a water pistol. He heads straight for the nearest sink so he can fill it up. His mother, looking displeased, turns to her mother and says, 'I'm surprised at you getting him something like that. Don't you remember how we used to drive you up the wall with water guns?' At which the older lady smiles and then replies, 'Oh yes, I remember!'

....

Children are a great comfort in your old age – and they help you reach it faster, too.

Lionel Kauffman

....

Wrinkles are hereditary. Parents get them from their children.

Doris Day

'Nanny, nanny, I'm so glad to see you!' the little boy says to his grandmother, 'Now Daddy will do the trick he's been promising us!'

'Oh?' His grandmother says,
'What trick is that?'

'He told mummy that he'd climb the walls the next time you came to visit,' says the little boy, grinning.

Blessed are the young, for they shall inherit the national debt.

Herbert Hoover

....

A young grandson decides to call his grandma and wish her happy birthday. While on the phone he asks, 'Grandma, how old are you now?' His grandma replies, 'I'm sixty-two years old now, son. It's been a long time coming.' After a slight pause, the grandson replies, 'Wow, Nan, that's a lot of years – did you start at one?'

....

What a bargain grandchildren are! I give them my loose change, and they give me a million dollars' worth of pleasure.

Gene Perret

The reason grandparents
and grandchildren get along
so well is that they have a
common enemy!

Margaret Mead

A young girl is at the deli counter buying some food for her dinner party. 'I'd like five hundred grams of that cheese,' she says, 'two hundred grams of the smoked ham and – how much is the caviar, please?'

'It's quite expensive I'm afraid – fifty pounds an ounce,' says the smooth-looking male server, 'but from a gorgeous girl like you I'd accept a kiss for each ounce you buy.'

'OK,' the girl says after a little thought, 'I'll take five ounces.' With an excited look the male server quickly measures out the caviar, wraps it up and holds it out suggestively for the girl. As he does, the girl quickly snatches the food. 'Thanks,' she says, and points to an elderly man beside her. 'My granddad said he'd pay.'

AND ANOTHER THING...

Old age is an excellent time for outrage. My goal is to say or do at least one outrageous thing every week.

Maggie Kuhn

I have a problem about being nearly sixty: I keep waking up in the morning and thinking I'm thirty-one.

Elizabeth Janeway

....

With sixty staring me in the face, I have developed inflammation of the sentence structure and a definite hardening of the paragraphs.

James Thurber

Inside every older person is a younger person – wondering what the hell happened.

Cora Harvey Armstrong

....

Audrey and Annabel are walking along the beachfront on a quiet Sunday afternoon, when all of a sudden a large seagull dropping lands on Audrey's shoulder. 'You see, Annabel,' she says angrily, 'this is why I don't come to the beach – too many undisciplined animals about! Do you have a tissue there dear, so I can sort this out?' 'Well, Audrey,' Annabel says, 'there doesn't seem to be much point – there's no way you'll get him to wipe his bum now, he's long gone!'

....

The surprising thing about young fools is how many survive to become old fools.

Doug Larson

By the time man is old enough to read a woman like a book, he's too old to start a library.

Anonymous

You can judge your age by the amount of pain you feel when you come in contact with a new idea.

Pearl S. Buck

....

Growing old is like being increasingly penalised for a crime you have not committed.

Anthony Powell

....

Women are not forgiven for ageing. Bob Redford's lines of distinction are my old age wrinkles.

Jane Fonda

When you are younger
you get blamed for
crimes you never
committed, and when
you're older you begin
to get credit for virtues
you never possessed.

I. F. STONE

I've travelled a long way, and some of the roads weren't paved.

Anonymous

....

There's nothing worse than being an ageing young person.

Richard Pryor

....

I would like to find a stew that will give me heartburn immediately, instead of at three o'clock in the morning.

John Barrymore

If I'd known how old I was going to be I'd have taken better care of myself.

Adolph Zukor

....

I'm fifty-nine and people call me middle-aged. How many 118-year-old men do you know?

Barry Cryer

....

Whatever poet, orator or sage may say of it, old age is still old age.

Sinclair Lewis

There was no respect for youth when I was young, and now that I am old, there is no respect for age — I missed it coming and going.

J. B. PRIESTLEY

The time to begin most things is ten years ago.

Mignon McLaughlin

....

By the time I have money to burn, my fire will have burnt out.

Anonymous

....

The first half of life consists of the capacity to enjoy without the chance; the last half consists of the chance without the capacity.

Mark Twain

You know you are getting old
when the candles cost more
than the cake.

Bob Hope

There is absolutely nothing to be said in favour of growing old. There ought to be legislation against it.

Patrick Moore

....

The older I get the better I used to be!

Lee Trevino

....

Youth would be an ideal state if it came a little later in life.

Herbert Asquith

The years between fifty and seventy are the hardest. You are always being asked to do more, and you are not yet decrepit enough to turn them down.

T. S. Eliot

....

Everything slows down with age, except the time it takes cake and ice cream to reach your hips.

John Wagner

....

The sign of old age is that I begin to philosophise and ponder over problems which should not be my concern at all.

Jawaharlal Nehru

I am old enough to see
how little I have done
in so much time, and
how much I have to do
in so little.

SHEILA KAYE-SMITH

An old couple, bored of having tea at their regular restaurant, decide they'd like to experience a bit of modern cuisine. So one night they head into the city and come across a trendy-looking restaurant – they walk in but are turned away as it's fully booked. 'I suggest, sir, that you call tomorrow to check if we've had any cancellations. You see, we're booked up for the next three weeks,' a haughty maître d' says. Feeling a little bemused, the couple return home.

The next evening they call the restaurant, but are told there have been no cancellations, and to try again another night.

After a week of calls, the old man has had enough and calls to complain: 'And let me give you some advice, sonny: trendy or not, you'd do a darn sight more business if you weren't so damn full all the time!'

KEEPING A TWINKLE IN YOUR WRINKLE

It's sad to grow old,
but nice to ripen.

Brigitte Bardot

I love everything that's old: old friends, old times, old manners, old books, old wines.

Oliver Goldsmith

....

With mirth and laughter let old wrinkles come.

William Shakespeare

....

None are so old as those who have outlived enthusiasm.

Henry David Thoreau

The best thing about getting old is that all those things you couldn't have when you were young you no longer want.

L. S. McCandless

....

One of the good things about getting older is you find you're more interesting than most of the people you meet.

Lee Marvin

....

Another belief of mine: that everyone else my age is an adult, whereas I am merely in disguise.

Margaret Atwood

Two senior men, both dragging their legs slightly, pass each other in the street. One says to the other, 'I can see we've both discovered the perils of old age... what happened to you?'

'Well,' the other man replies, 'this is an old war wound coming back to haunt me. Took some shrapnel in the leg at Normandy, 'forty-four. What's your story?'

'Me?' says the other man, 'Got a problem with my foot. I trod in some dog muck a couple of streets back.'

I'm not denying my age, I'm embellishing my youth.

Tamara Reynolds

....

I've only got one wrinkle and I'm sitting on it.

Jeanne Calment

I'm saving that rocker for the day when I feel as old as I really am.

Dwight D. Eisenhower

....

You're never too old to become younger.

Mae West

....

I was always taught to respect my elders and I've now reached the age when I don't have anybody to respect.

George Burns

Growing old is mandatory;
growing up is optional.

Chili Davis

Age is something that doesn't matter, unless you are a cheese.

Billie Burke

....

To get back my youth I would do anything in the world, except take exercise, get up early, or be respectable.

Oscar Wilde

....

You're not old. You're classic.

Anonymous

A man's only as old as the woman
he feels.

Groucho Marx

....

Age is an issue of mind over matter. If
you don't mind, it doesn't matter.

Mark Twain

....

There is no pleasure worth forgoing
just for an extra three years in the
geriatric ward.

John Mortimer

A reporter is interviewing a group of senior citizens for a newspaper feature entitled 'Super Seniors'. The reporter asks one lady what the secret to her youthful appearance is, to which she replies, 'I think a little bit of everything is the best way to stay healthy and happy. If you do things in moderation, you can't go far wrong.'

'But madam,' the reporter replies, 'Your daughter told us earlier that you have, on several occasions, been seriously ill as a result of your lifestyle.'

'Well, yes,' the woman replies. 'But you can't very well put that in the article can you?'

Grow old with me! The best is yet to be.

Robert Browning

....

**I don't want my wrinkles taken away –
I don't want to look like everyone else.**

Jane Fonda

....

**I'm not interested in age. People who tell
me their age are silly. You're as old
as you feel.**

Elizabeth Arden

The ageing process has you firmly in its grasp if you never get the urge to throw a snowball.

Doug Larson

Sometimes age succeeds, sometimes it fails. It depends on you.

Ravensara Noite

....

To be seventy years young is sometimes far more cheerful and hopeful than to be forty years old.

Oliver Wendell Holmes

....

I didn't get old on purpose, it just happened. If you're lucky, it could happen to you.

Andy Rooney

A man is not old as long as he is seeking something.

Jean Rostand

....

Live your life and forget your age.

Norman Vincent Peale

....

He has a profound respect for old age. Especially when it's bottled.

Gene Fowler

After avoiding it for several years, a retired man decides to bring himself into the modern age and get a computer. His young grandson, a dab hand at using the Internet, decides to help him get to grips with surfing the World Wide Web. 'What's this search engine thing, then?' the old man asks. 'It's great, Granddad,' the grandson replies, 'you just ask it a question and it gives you the answer. You can find out anything!'
'Anything, eh?' the old man says, types 'What will next week's winning lottery numbers be?' and hits 'SEARCH'.

While there's snow on the roof,
it doesn't mean the fire has gone out
in the furnace.

John G. Diefenbaker

....

I've got it two ways: I'm still making
movies, and I'm a senior citizen, so I can
see myself at half price.

George Burns

....

Don't act your age. Act like the inner
young person you have always been.

J. A. West

Cherish all your happy moments: they make a fine cushion for old age.

Christopher Marley

....

As a senior citizen, you may as well learn to laugh at yourself. Everyone else is.

Judy Huffman

....

Ageing is a privilege, not a predicament.

Anonymous

There is no old age.
There is, as there always
was, just you.

CAROL MATTHAU

A WORD TO THE WIZENED

Wisdom doesn't necessarily come with age. Sometimes age just shows up all by itself.

Tom Wilson

Don't let ageing get you down. It's too hard to get back up.

John Wagner

....

At a local cafe, a young woman is telling her friends about her idea of the perfect partner. 'The man I marry should be a shining light in company. He must be musical. Tell jokes. Entertain. And stay at home with me at night!' An old lady overhears and decides to speak up: 'Pardon me for saying so, but after a lifetime's experience I can say with confidence that if that's all you want, I would advise getting a TV!'

The gardener's rule applies to youth and age: when young sow wild oats, but when old, grow sage.

H. J. Byron

....

What is the most common remark made by sixty-year-olds when they browse in an antiques shop?

I remember these.

....

Old age... It is true you are gently shouldered off the stage, but then you are given such a comfortable front stall as spectator.

Jane Harrison

Age does not diminish the extreme disappointment of having a scoop of ice cream fall from the cone.

Jim Fiebig

....

A woman past forty should make up her mind to be young; not her face.

Billie Burke

An old man is walking past a group of teenagers who are all laughing uncontrollably. The man is intrigued and so asks what the joke is. 'Well, if you must know,' one boy explains, 'we're seeing who can tell the biggest lie about their sex life.' With a look of disgust the old man says, 'You lot should be ashamed of yourselves! When I was your age the thought of sex hadn't even crossed my mind!' To which the boy replies, 'OK old timer, you win!'

Don't worry about avoiding temptation –
as you grow older, it starts avoiding you.

Anonymous

....

Middle age is when you go to bed at night
and hope you feel better in the morning.
Old age is when you go to bed at night
and hope you wake up in the morning.

Groucho Marx

....

Of course I have regrets, but if you are
sixty years old and you have no regrets
then you haven't lived.

Christy Moore

Anyone who stops learning is old,
whether at twenty or eighty.

Henry Ford

....

Old age isn't so bad when you
consider the alternative.

Maurice Chevalier

....

We are only young once. That is
all society can stand.

Bob Bowen

The key to successful ageing is to pay as little attention to it as possible.

JUDITH REGAN

An old gent is backing his Rolls-Royce into the last available parking space, when a young guy in a brand new sports car zips into the spot. The young driver jumps out and says, 'Sorry old boy, but you've got to be young and smart to do that.' The old man ignores the snide remark and keeps reversing until his Rolls crushes the back of the sports car into an unrecognisable mess. 'Sorry son, you've got to be old and rich to do that!'

You know you're getting old when you get to that one candle on the cake. It's like, 'See if you can blow this out.'

Jerry Seinfeld

....

A person is always startled when he hears himself seriously called an old man for the first time.

Oliver Wendell Holmes

A man asks his father how he feels about reaching his sixty-fifth birthday. 'Well son, I've worked hard all my life, and to be honest, I don't feel like I've got much to show for it.' Seeing that his question had saddened the old man, the son decides to lighten the mood: 'But dad, what with the silver in your hair, the gold in your teeth and the gas in your stomach, you're worth a small fortune!'

....

Old age is like a plane flying through a storm. Once you're abroad, there's nothing you can do.

Golda Meir

True terror is to wake up one morning and discover that your high-school class is running the country.

Kurt Vonnegut

....

Age is whatever you think it is. You are as old as you think you are.

Muhammad Ali

....

There are people whose watch stops at a certain hour and who remain permanently at that age.

Charles Augustin Sainte-Beuve

They only name things after you when you're dead or really old.

GEORGE H. W. BUSH

If you survive long enough, you're revered – rather like an old building.

Katharine Hepburn

Old men are fond of giving good advice,
to console themselves for being no
longer in a position to give bad examples.

François La Rochefoucauld

. . . .

You must become an old man soon if you
would be an old man long.

Roman proverb

. . . .

The older I grow the more I distrust the
familiar doctrine that age brings wisdom.

H. L. Mencken

I'm going to be eighty soon, and I guess the one thing that puzzles me most is how quick it got here.

Roy Acuff

....

Age is not different from earlier life as long as you're sitting down.

Malcolm Cowley

....

Old age is ready to undertake tasks that youth shirked because they would take too long.

W. Somerset Maugham

An inordinate passion for pleasure is the secret of remaining young.

Oscar Wilde

Forty is the old age of youth; fifty the youth of old age.

Victor Hugo

....

We are always the same age inside.

Gertrude Stein

....

It is not how old you are, but how you are old.

Marie Dressler

A concerned senior lady visits her doctor to check her health. After her examination, the doctor tells her that she's in good health. 'Good enough to live till a hundred?' she asks. 'Well,' says the doctor, 'you don't smoke, do you?' 'No,' she says. 'And you don't drink?' Again the answer is no. 'And you don't have a frivolous and excessive lifestyle, taking advantage of every moment to enjoy yourself?' 'Not at all,' the lady says. 'In that case,' the doctor says, 'why on earth would you want to live to a hundred?!'

Old age ain't no place for sissies.

Bette Davis

....

You're only as young as the last time you changed your mind.

Timothy Leary

....

If you think nobody cares if you're alive, try missing a couple of car payments.

Flip Wilson

In three words I can
sum up everything I've
learned about life:
it goes on.

ROBERT FROST

If you're interested in finding out more about our books,
find us on Facebook at **Summersdale Publishers** and
follow us on Twitter at **@Summersdale**.

www.summersdale.com